MARY BAKER EDDY

A SPECIAL FRIEND

The text for this book was expanded from the article, "Mary Baker Eddy—her life and special place," which was published in the *Christian Science Sentinel*, September 1, 1980.

Library of Congress Catalog Card Number : 83–072002

ISBN 0–87510–165–8

MARY BAKER EDDY
A SPECIAL FRIEND

Karin Sass
illustrated by **Christa Kieffer**

The Christian Science Publishing Society
Boston, Massachusetts, U.S.A.

WHEN Mary Baker Eddy was a little girl, she learned about

the people in the Bible. She loved to hear about David

and Joseph and Daniel and all the others. Best of all she loved to learn

about Christ Jesus and his disciples. Every day the family gathered to listen
to Father reading the Bible. In those days, even though many people read
about the wonderful things that Jesus did, no one knew how he did them.

Mary and her five older brothers and sisters lived with their mother
and father and grandmother on a busy farm. Mary loved to play outdoors
and help take care of the animals. Sometimes she would take special care
of a lamb that was ill and nurse it back to health.

The school Mary went to was a long walk from her house, and it had only one room. All the children, big and small, sat together there. Albert, Mary's big brother, taught her at home, too.

Mary was happy when she learned to read. Her favorite thing to do was to find a quiet place where she could be alone with the books she liked. She especially loved reading the Bible.

One day when Mary was twelve years old, she became very ill.
Mary's mother knew that God loved His children. She told Mary to lean
on God's love and to pray to Him. Mary did this, and she was quickly well
again. This made Mary and her mother very happy. Because she had been
healed when she prayed, Mary began to see that God could help and heal.

As Mary grew up, her sisters married, and they and her brothers left home. Mary also married and went to live far away. Before long, however, her husband became ill and died. Mary was going to have a baby, and she went back home to live with her mother and father.

A few months later her baby boy was born.

Mary taught school sometimes and wrote poems and stories

to earn money, but she was often ill. She loved her little boy, George,

very much, but sometimes she needed someone else to take care of him.

When George was about six years old, he went to live with Mahala

and Russell Cheney. Mahala loved George, too; and took good care of him. In a few years the Cheneys moved away and George went with them. But Mary never stopped praying for her son, knowing that God would take care of him.

Many years later Mary heard from her son. He said he would come

to see her, too. They loved each other.

Mary was kind to people and liked being with her friends. One evening she went to a meeting with some of them. It was the winter of 1866, and there was ice on the ground. Mary slipped on the ice and was badly hurt.

Mary's friends thought she would die. But three days after her fall, she opened her Bible and turned to a story about Jesus healing a man who could not walk. As she read, she suddenly saw that God is Life and that His love is everywhere. She was healed at that moment.

After this, Mary wanted to know more about how Jesus had healed
so many people and how she herself had been healed. She spent
much time studying the Bible and praying, seeking to know God better.
She learned how God heals, so that she was able to heal others. To share
what she had learned, she wrote a book about it and named her book
Science and Health with Key to the Scriptures.

Mary called her discovery Christian Science because it was based on what Christ Jesus said and did and it could be proved by healing. She did all she could to help people know more about Christian Science. She healed and taught and wrote about it too.

A little boy named Stanley who was often stubborn and naughty lived in the same town as Mary. He got very sick. His mother became frightened and took him to Mary for healing. Mary prayed deeply. She understood that God is good and loving and that He did not make sickness.

Soon Stanley sat up and said, "I is tick." Mary told Stanley,

"You are not sick, and you are a good boy." Soon, Stanley was well,

and from then on he behaved better, too.

When Mary's son George came to see her, he was grown-up

and had a family of his own. George had named his little girl Mary,

after his mother. But he said that the little girl was cross-eyed.

His mother told him that wasn't true about her. Mary knew

that God loved her little granddaughter as He did all His children.

God had made her perfect, not cross-eyed. "Her eyes are all right,"

she told George. When he returned home, he found his daughter's eyes

had been healed.

Before Mary Baker Eddy did anything she would pray to God and listen closely for His answer. The Bible sometimes calls God "Shepherd," and Mrs. Eddy liked to think of Him that way. She always prayed to be guided by God, and wrote a poem that is a prayer which begins

Shepherd, show me how to go
O'er the hillside steep,
How to gather, how to sow,—
How to feed Thy sheep;
I will listen for Thy voice,
Lest my footsteps stray;
I will follow and rejoice
All the rugged way.

When more and more people were becoming interested in her discovery, Mrs. Eddy prayed to know how to organize her Church. The answer was to have a main church, The First Church of Christ, Scientist, in Boston, Massachusetts. All the others would be branch churches. The rules Mrs. Eddy wrote for her church are called By-Laws. They are in the *Manual of The Mother Church*.

One rule says that every church shall have a Reading Room where anyone can study or borrow or buy the Bible, *Science and Health*, and other books from The Mother Church. Another rule gives us the Sunday School, where we learn about God and Christ Jesus and how to heal.

Mrs. Eddy started three magazines to help people learn more about her discovery. When she started a newspaper, someone tried to talk her out of publishing it. She said, "God calls upon me to found a daily newspaper."

And she went right on. When her newspaper, *The Christian Science Monitor*, came out she said it would help the whole world. It does.

Mrs. Eddy wanted everyone to listen first of all to God. She said, "Trust God to direct your steps. Accept my counsel and teachings only as they include the spirit and the letter of the Ten Commandments, the Beatitudes, and the teachings and example of Christ Jesus."[1]

[1] *The First Church of Christ, Scientist, and Miscellany*, p. 129.

Like an explorer who finds a wonderful land that no one else knows about, Mary Baker Eddy found Christian Science. That is why she is very special. She knew that Jesus wanted us to do the things that he did.

Though she lived many years ago, Mrs. Eddy is still teaching us through her writings how very much God loves us and how we can heal through prayer. That is why we love her as the Discoverer and Founder of Christian Science. And that is also why we call her our Leader.